GEO

Stringed Instruments

Music Makers

THE CHILD'S WORLD®, INC.

Stringed Instruments

Kathryn Stevens

THE CHILD'S WORLD®, INC.

Stringed Instruments

Music is all around us—on the radio, on television, and performed live. Wherever you find people playing music, you'll find stringed instruments.

Stringed instruments have strings or wires that are stretched tight. Plucking, rubbing, or tapping the strings makes a sound. Stringed instruments come in many different kinds—and they make just as many different sounds!

← These people are playing stringed instruments on a front porch in Tennessee.

How Do Stringed Instruments Make Sounds?

If you stretch a rubber band tight and pluck it with your fingers, it makes a sound. The rubber band makes the sound as it moves rapidly back and forth, or **vibrates**.

You can make the sound louder by holding one end against a hollow box. The box vibrates along with the string, or **resonates**. The string and the box make a louder sound when they vibrate together. Most stringed instruments have a hollow body that is made to resonate.

The strings of a guitar run over a hole in the instrument's ➡️ body. The body makes the sound louder.

Tuning Stringed Instruments

A string makes a higher or lower sound, or **pitch**, depending on how fast it vibrates. A short, thin, or tight string vibrates fast and has a high pitch. A long, thick, or loose string vibrates slower and has a lower pitch.

Most stringed instruments have some thicker strings and some thinner ones. The thinner strings can be tuned higher. You tune each string by turning a peg. The peg winds the string tighter to raise its pitch and loosens it to lower its pitch.

← You can see the six tuning pegs on this guitar.

How Are Stringed Instruments Played?

You play many stringed instruments by plucking the strings with your fingers. For a sharper, crisper sound, you can use a hard **pick** made of plastic or metal. Other stringed instruments are played with a long wooden **bow**. The bow has hairs stretched between the ends. Rubbing the bow across the strings makes a long, steady sound.

This man is playing an *er-hu*, a traditional Chinese stringed instrument. →

While one hand makes the strings move, the other hand holds the strings against the long, skinny part of the instrument (called the neck). Holding the strings against the neck makes different notes—but how? Holding down a string makes the vibrating part shorter. The shortened string produces a higher sound. Pressing the strings down in one spot after another creates lots of different sounds, or **notes**.

Here you can see how this musician uses ➡ his fingers to create notes on a guitar.

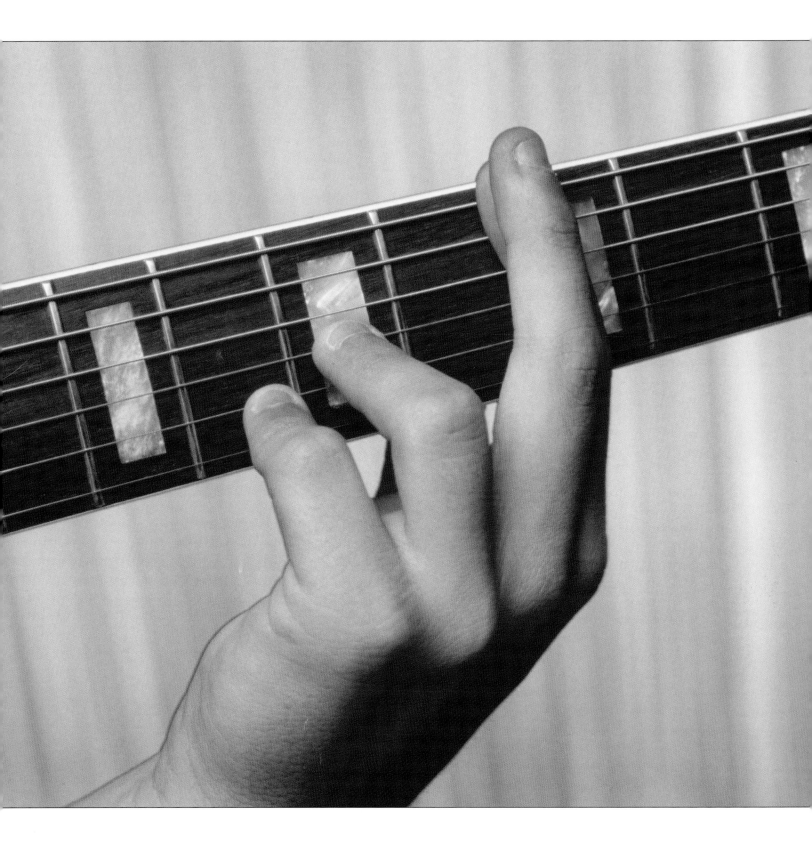

The Violin Family

Some of the best-known stringed instruments are the members of the violin family. The violin is the smallest in this group. The larger viola has a slightly deeper sound. The much bigger cello has a lower, richer sound. Biggest of all is the double bass. The violin family is an important part of any orchestra.

To play a violin or viola, you tuck it under your chin. Cellos and double basses are too big to tuck under your chin! Instead, you must stand them upright.

← This boy is holding his violin under his chin while he plays.

Guitars

Guitars are popular for everything from quiet orchestral music to loud rock and roll. To play a guitar, you strum or pluck the strings with one hand while your other hand holds down certain strings. Playing several strings at once produces a **chord**.

Some guitars are connected by wires to an electric **amplifier**. The amplifier works somewhat like a radio or a stereo. The amplifier's speakers make the guitar sound louder. Many rock, jazz, and blues musicians use electric guitars.

This boy is playing chords on his guitar. ➡

20

The elegant harp is a very different kind of stringed instrument. A harp has many strings. Each string is a different length and plays a different note. Some harps have foot pedals that can stretch the strings to produce even more notes. To play a harp, you hold it upright and pluck the strings with your fingers.

Pianos

Pianos are stringed instruments, too, but they work differently from violins, guitars, and harps. Pianos have a **keyboard**. Each key on the keyboard plays a different string. When you press the key, a hammer inside the piano hits the string and makes a sound. Some other keyboard instruments, such as harpsichords, pluck the strings instead of hitting them.

Pianos and other stringed instruments are lots of fun to play. Would you like to learn how to play a stringed instrument?

Here a piano maker pulls strings tightly into place. ➜

Glossary

amplifier (AM-plih-fy-er)
An amplifier is a device that takes a sound and makes it louder. Some kinds of guitars are connected to an amplifier.

bow (BOH)
A bow is a long piece of wood with hairs stretched between the ends. Some stringed instruments are played by rubbing a bow across the strings.

chord (KORD)
A chord is a group of notes played at the same time. Guitars and many other stringed instruments can be used to play chords.

keyboard (KEE-bord)
A keyboard is a panel of buttons or levers that you push to make something happen. Pianos have a keyboard, and each key plays a different string.

notes (NOHTS)
Notes are sounds in music. Stringed instruments can make lots of different notes.

pick (PICK)
In music, a pick is a hard piece of plastic or metal used to pluck or strum the strings of an instrument. Picks produce a sharper, harder sound than plucking the strings with your fingers.

pitch (PITCH)
In music, pitch is how high or low a sound is. On stringed instruments, a string's pitch depends on how tight, long, or thick the string is.

resonates (REZ-uh-nates)
When something resonates, it vibrates and fills with sound. On stringed instruments, the whole body of the instrument resonates along with the moving strings.

vibrates (VY-brates)
When something vibrates, it moves back and forth very quickly. If you pluck or rub a tightly stretched string, it vibrates and makes a sound.

Index